ASHES AT MY GURU'S FEET

ASHES
AT MY GURU'S FEET

POEMS BY

GURUMAYI
CHIDVILASANANDA

PUBLISHED BY SYDA FOUNDATION

Published by SYDA Foundation®
P.O. Box 600, South Fallsburg, New York 12779, U.S.A.

ACKNOWLEDGEMENTS

The contribution of everyone who helped to prepare this book for
publication is deeply appreciated. Our thanks go to George Franklin
and Jane Ferrar for their selection of the poetry, to Cynthia Kline
who supervised production, to Kathie Kemp for her design,
to William Shirley for his illustrations, and to all those
who offered their services with great love.

Swami Kripananda

Library of Congress Cataloging-in-Publication Data

Chidvilasananda, Gurumayi.
    Ashes at my Guru's feet : poems / Gurumayi Chidvilasananda.
       p.   cm.
    ISBN 0-911307-16-8
    1. Spiritual life--Poetry.   2. Yoga, Siddha--Poetry.   3. Siddhas-
-Poetry.   I. Title.
PS3553.H475A84   1990
811'.54--dc20   90-30300
                                              CIP

Printed in Hong Kong

CONTENTS

ILLUSTRATIONS

THE SIDDHA LINEAGE

The lineage of Siddhas is imperishable and timeless, a legacy of divine wisdom flowing down through the ages. In this century, the revered Siddha, Bhagawan Nityananda, wandered the length and breadth of India. In his presence, suffering was alleviated and questions dissolved. Spontaneously, people's minds would come to rest, and they found themselves experiencing the highest spiritual states. Bhagawan Nityananda settled at last on holy ground on the banks of a river, and a village grew around him. Ganeshpuri, this ancient ground, is the home of Siddha Yoga.

Bhagawan Nityananda's beloved disciple, Swami Muktananda Paramahamsa, was chosen to carry the greatness of his Guru throughout India and the West. For the first time in history, Baba Muktananda made the initiation of the Siddhas available to everyone. Baba was an extraordinary being. In him were united the known and the unknown, the exalted and the practical, the seen and the unseen. In time, Baba Muktananda chose his own successor, a being like himself. He prepared and tested her from childhood. Then he gave her what his Guru had given him. The ancient power, perfect knowledge, and sacred authority of the Siddhas were passed on to Gurumayi Chidvilasananda.

Gurumayi has walked the path from beginning to end and knows its shadows and light. Established in that state of bliss and freedom which is the final goal, such a Master guides our

every step along the way. Gurumayi is a Siddha Master, a
perfected disciple who has been commanded and empowered to
bestow the grace of an unbroken lineage of Siddhas. These great
beings are an ocean of compassion, a shoreless sea of light. They
recreate the original insight of the whole spiritual tradition.
They are scripture and mantra. They turn this very world into
a paradise.

PREFACE

Speech becomes The Word when spoken by a saint, as the following collection of Gurumayi's poems shows. Long awaited, these poems exceed all expectations. We have heard that "A poem should not mean, but Be." But here, from every page and line, both meaning and the experience of pure being unfold. Again and again I am suspended in midstream, overwhelmed by the teachings of her Word. Enlightenment is embedded in every syllable.

> *All times are God's time,*
> *And God's time is eternity.*

So simple a couplet stops my mind. I reel and call for time out to contemplate so pure a gem, tossed casually among a rolling surge of revelation. As common tools become uncommon in the hands of genius, a poem springing from the heart of God transcends all boundaries of tongue, carries us beyond all words, yet tells us everything there is to know. Like the Guru herself, each poem is a state unto itself, whole and self-sufficient, yet an endless fountain of wisdom and delight. Where else have we found the truth of the heart springing in such lyric form as this:

> *As the light comes streaming down,*
> *Yesterday, today, and forever,*
> *The air is draped with a white robe.*
> *The rivers seem to flow with milk.*
> *The entire Earth rejoices*
> *With the tenderness of love . . .*

Lyrics pour in cascades here, singing as clearly as brook on stone; lines as perfect as a flower carved in jade. Opening our mind and heart to them, we find she gives us yet another way to share her radiant state.

Narratives are here as well, full poetic sagas that echo the lives of all the saints. Gurumayi's is the story of our species' struggle for transcendence; she reflects the spiritual striving of us all. As the honest man is said to need no memory — since all he says stands in its truth and needs no defensive reflection — so the purity of a saint has nothing to hide. With the freedom of being one with Him, Gurumayi reveals her sadhana to us, in all its joys and sorrows, pains and ecstasies. In this, her most charitable gift, we find that she has gone through and beyond more trials and tears than we may ever know.

The house of my individuality was set ablaze . . .

she writes, in a brilliant display of metaphor, the language of true poetry. Spinning this metaphor out with skill she says:

I wanted to save my house.

So simple a line, it holds the plight of ages. And then, she quietly draws the tension of our all-too-human desire.

When that was impossible,
I wanted to save a few possessions.

My secret cache of last desires is unearthed here — those

"few possessions" that become the massive stumble. But
Gurumayi finds:

> *I could not escape —*
> *The door of the house was also on fire.*

There is no exit from that love which saves us from our selves.

She writes of the "thousand mirrors on the table of my life,"
and shares with us the shattering of each when Guru's grace has
struck. "Destruction took its time" she tells us, in that economy
of speech that all great poetry displays. "Destruction took its
time;" the shattering was slow, but absolutely thorough. And
although "My whole being wept. My senses abandoned me," still
"My world crumbled . . ." until "The last mirror, which gave
me hope . . . support . . . held my universe together . . .
exploded." Then "Not even a trace remained of that existence
which had once found meaning in reflections." And are not we,
caught in pale reflections, equally caught in longing for that
clear light she found?

Through every page runs her recurrent theme: the way to
that pure light is through pure love. She sings of her Guru's
purifying love, and moves to purify ours in turn, that we may
see as she sees:

> *You must have devoted eyes,*
> *Vision that is pure enough to perceive*
> *The light that is constantly streaming down.*

The truth of all the saints rings steady here: the light of God is within us all. As William Blake has said, we need but "cleanse the doors of our perception" to behold that light. Gurumayi's love is that cleansing fire. "The form that I can always love . . ." she tells us, ". . . takes me to the formless."

The power of poetry is said to be its ability to "suggest without compelling." Through gentle nuance, through the subtlest shift of tone, Gurumayi opens an unsung ocean of delight and sorrow, if we can but hear the space within her words. A hint of exultation, a silent sigh, will loom fleeting and inarticulate, waiting for our hidden resonance to make it our own. Consider:

Baba, your sweet fire sings its song
In the space of my heart,

rapturous lines which make more poignant the sharp thrust of so simple an aside as:

O my Baba . . .
I never believed that I would be here
And you would be there.
Destiny has played an inscrutable game.

She has known our sorrows at first hand yet celebrates a joy that transcends all grief. Scorning self-pity she accepts that inscrutable game of destiny's unknowing, and rises above and goes beyond the shadow side of love. Only one who has gone through the fire of discipleship can be so perfect a master and guide. In poem after poem, with a candor and clarity so simple they are compelling, she describes that refining fire.

I was handed these poems as I left for the airport, off on my perpetual circuit of talks, so I read them first at 35,000 feet. An appropriate setting. Time and again lines arose which forced me to pause and gather myself, gazing down at far away greens and browns, voluminous clouds around. I saw that all was Gurumayi's ashram, the living globe her gift, these poems a song for the whole earth. I saw this volume as my life-long study, all I'll ever need, each reading opening me to more and more. I'll never get enough. As in all her ways of giving, again she gives her all. Even a fragment can tell us all there is to know.

So don't pass by this treasure casually, nor read through it lightly. Within these songs and sagas lie universal depths, the depths of knowing and unknowing — inviting, foreboding, challenging.

Drinking this love
Gurumayi sings,
Sometimes I drown, sometimes I soar.
Yet there is no touching bottom nor reaching the top.

May we, immersed in her Word, drown and soar with her, in this, her expression of fathomless love.

Joseph Chilton Pearce
Oakland, California
May 16, 1989

PART ONE

Jaya Guru Muktananda!

THE FIRE OF MY LOVE

The fire of my love blazes through
The crystal of my heart.
Just picture the colorful patterns of the fiery flames.
Just imagine the heat of the fire's brilliant blaze.

When that fire of love is reflected through
The crystal of my heart,
You can imagine what its glory must be
And how divine a sight it is.

You know my love exists for you;
And when you touch it,
Its patterns sweep through my entire being.

Every pore of my body is a spark of love for you.

I AM NOT THE SAME

I was warned about the flames of love . . .
This love is merciless; it ravages your heart.
From its heat you become wild and mad.
So mysterious is its energy that when it seizes you,
You become impassioned and run about frenzied.
People sense in you the sparks of love,
But they cannot see the raging fire within.
This love is tantalizing. It wholly possesses you;
It does not fill your heart and mind alone.
How it courses through every cell of your being!
It is brighter than lightning;
It is more deafening than thunder;
It pours over you more intensely than a cloudburst.
You can fantasize endlessly about love.
But remember: you can never bend it to your will.
It is independent, very free, very free.
Having known all its intricacies and madness,
I still dived into the flames of love.
I cannot say what has happened to me, except
     I am not the same,
     I am not the same,
     I am not the same.

MY BEING HAS BECOME YOU

What a beautiful moment it was
When you looked into my eyes.
There was something in that look —
What was it? Were you aware of it?
It was powerful, yet very tender —
Beyond the grasp of this world.
Later you told me it was love.
You took me by surprise;
Still, I understood it was my destiny.
Yes, your love is my destiny.
Having known only its surface,
Now I yearn to plumb its depths.
Perhaps it is unfathomable.
Every pore of the body, mind, and heart
Must be saturated with it.
I stay here; but no, no, I live with you,
And you fill me with your love.
Do you know it is your love
That pours out of me?
My being has become you.
Baba, you are my love.
My heart throbs with the pulsation
Of your love.

NO WONDER
THAT I LOVE YOU!

Baba, I give thanks to God
For having your form incarnate on this earth.
Through your form, I have come to love
The most elusive nature of God.

As I began my search, your form was my inspiration.
Whenever I lost trust, your form was still ablaze
With the light of God; and so I would begin again,
And would continue my search with greater faith.

As your sweet, enchanting form became my goal,
An incredible thing happened — I disappeared.
As I went still deeper into you, form itself dissolved;
Nothing remained but light — boundless, radiant light!
No color, no sound, no touch, no smell, no taste survived.
Beyond the grasp of the senses, nothing was left to describe;
The sole reality was the experience of God.
Once again, an incredible thing happened —
As I came to, the light of God condensed into your form.

O my Baba, you are God incarnate in a human form —
No wonder, no wonder that I love you!

THOU ART THAT

My Guru is the fire of love.
His look, his word, his touch, his will
Shoot lightning throughout my being.

When I feel that his look has erased me,
I am struck by his word,
And I realize that there is still further to go;
When I believe that there is nothing more,
I am blessed with his touch;
When I think that there is no more of me,
The fire of his will immolates me.

At times his love is too great to bear.
The breath goes wild within me.
Thoughts become scattered, and the moods
That underlie action have no aim, no destination.

I wonder: "What will all this accomplish?
Is there any hope?
Is there any meaning?
Is there any purpose?"

I watch the blazing fire of his love
Consume every particle within and without,
And am left with nothing.

Then once again his look, his word,
His touch, and his will
Mold me into the form of his love.
It is evident that the fire of that love
Is both the destroyer and the creator.

The Guru reduces you to ashes through his love,
And then molds you into pearls of wisdom,
Pearls of dignity, pearls of surrender,
Pearls of tenderness and beauty;

Finally, he absorbs all the pearls into one
Called the Blue Pearl.

Then he gives you back to yourself,
Saying, "Thou art That."

LOVE'S SWEET FIRE

Through the fire of love, O my Baba,
You keep me pure and close to you.
I never believed that I would be here
And you would be there.
Destiny has played an inscrutable game.
But, O my Baba, through the fire of love
You sustain me in your own effulgent being.
Your love gives force to my breathing,
To my speaking, to my very life.
It is your love that holds me together
In this disintegrating world
And in the world of Truth.

The Upanishads glorify your love.
The scriptures point to your love.
But the fire of your love is self-evident.
It is its own teaching, its own song.

O my Baba, you are so merciful!
All else will vanish, but your love will remain.
Your love is nectar; your love is life;
Your love is immortality.

The fire of your love
Creates form and dissolves it,
Gives rise to thought and dissolves it.
Brings about action and dissolves it.

Discrimination and detachment
Are the two tongues of the fire of your love.
As this fire blazes eternally in my heart,
I watch countless sparks leap out of it
And fall back into it.
When this is the case,
What is action, and what is inaction?

Baba, your sweet fire sings its song
In the space of my heart.
Your sweet fire dances its dance
In the palace of my heart.
Your sweet fire of love conceals itself
In the cave of my heart.

May your grace always protect this fire of love;
May your grace always nurture it.
O Baba, never separate me from your sweet fire.

No more existence! No more separation!
All that is, is nothing
But the blazing flame of your love.

You are my love.
Love is you.
What else is there but love?

MY PRAYER TO BABA

O Baba, let me live forever in the universe
In which you dwell. Never leave me,
And never allow me to leave you.
With your grace, Baba, may I always breathe
The air that you breathe. With your grace
May I always see what you see.
With your grace, Baba, may I walk
The same path that you walk. May I be lost
In the love of my Guru, just as you are lost
In the love of yours.
O Baba, to live in a universe other than yours
Would be worse than living in hell.

I know that my Guru has heard my prayer.
He has given me everything I wish for.
He has miraculously transformed himself
Into the subtlest, most divine love
That can ever exist in this universe.
Drinking this love, sometimes I drown,
Sometimes I soar.
Yet there is no touching bottom
Nor reaching the top.
O Baba, all that exists is your love,
The love of my Guru, the love that is you.

LIFE OF MY LIFE

You have understood me
Just as I understand myself;
Yet you have known me
As I have never known myself.
You are great. I understand this
As you work through me;
Yet you are greater than great,
For you escape the reaches
Of my understanding.
You are my feelings,
But you are not limited.
You are my thoughts,
But you are not transitory.
You are my actions,
But you are not bound.
You want me to know you
In the way I must know you.
You change nothing, though changes
Keep taking place.
You are so detached,
And yet, O life of my life,
I cannot stop loving you.

HAPPY THANKSGIVING DAY

God is so kind, yet people
Tend to forget His generosity.
For this reason He has created
Some grateful people
To remind the forgetful ones
That His abundant blessings
Are the source of everyone's life.

Thanking God is indispensable.
When you give thanks to God
Enormous joy flows through your life.
The happier you grow inside
The brighter your world becomes.
And finally, you feel God's love everywhere.

I thank God for my Guru, Muktananda,
And I thank my Guru for the God
He has revealed within me.

But I hear my Guru laughing —
Why does he laugh?
Perhaps he wants to see how I will thank him.
Yes, he is right. He is me, I am him;
When this is the case
Who is going to thank whom?

And yet there is such great grace
In loving and thanking my Guru
That I want to be separate from him
Though always remembering we are one.

O Baba, you are the *rasa* of my life.
Your love is the light of my life.
O Baba, you are love itself.

Thank you, thank you, thank you.

GURU PURNIMA

Guru Purnima,
The celebration of all celebrations,
Is the day devoted exclusively to the Guru.
All days and nights are nothing but the pulsation
Of the Guru's Shakti.
And yet, O my beloved Guru Muktananda,
Guru Purnima is that day and night
When even the moon reveals its full luster,
When all days and nights
Have reached their culmination
And are in suspension,
Awaiting a glimpse of their own Master.

O Guru Muktananda,
Though you are the embodiment
Of all that divine energy,
Though you carried the message
Of your own Gurudev, Bhagawan Nityananda,
Though you imparted all the teachings
To everyone who came before you or thought of you,
Who saw your picture, read your books, or dreamt of you,

Never for a moment did you stop showing your gratitude
To your own beloved Guru. All that you did
You attributed to the grace of Bhagawan Nityananda.
You considered yourself a blade of grass
In the court of your Guru.
Such humility, such divine love, such surrender!
No wonder you became everything
That thousands of people experienced within themselves.

Today is the most auspicious day.
It is so divinely auspicious because of your existence.
You are the Guru who transforms
Even nothing into everything good.
Your presence makes this day even more special.
Your existence makes every day worth living.
Your knowledge and your wisdom make life resplendent.

You loved this day above all others
When you lived on earth in a physical body,
Because you could show more gratitude to your Guru.
Your whole being was the worship of Bhagawan Nityananda.
You sang for him, you talked for him,
You cooked for him, you dressed for him.

You have made the Guru's Shakti come alive.
Although the Guru's Shakti is constantly pulsating,
Somehow you infuse it with even more *prana*.

On the day of Guru Purnima, you looked like Lord Shiva.
You revealed something unique and secret
To those who had the eyes to perceive.
You imparted the Guru's Shakti
Even more obviously than at other times.
You brought out more devotion to the Guru,
Even in the driest of hearts.

What a name you have!
The sweetest name — Muktananda.
I can live just singing your name,
Muktananda, Muktananda, O my beloved Muktananda!

I want to garland you,
But where can I find the flowers
Which are not already yours?

I want to wrap you in a warm shawl,
But what can be warmer than your own being?

I want to adorn you with the most beautiful sandals,
But how can I make any sandals fit *So'ham*,
Which are your feet?

I want to wave the lights for you,
But will I see that flame before your effulgence?

You are so great and so divine,
How can I do anything for you?
You are everything I see, hear, taste, and touch.
You are everywhere I go.
You are universal Being,
That vibrating, scintillating, dynamic Shakti.

If you ever wish to become very small,
Then let me know so I can play with you.
Otherwise, on this day of Guru Purnima,
I can only offer my salutations to you in all directions.

May the wind carry my message to you,
May the fire illumine it,
May the water keep it moist,
May the earth keep it solid,
And the ether keep it pure.

O my sweet Muktananda!
Seated within,
It is you who make me say all this.
What must I do?

You are the inspiration of my life,
Which has been offered at your feet.

Jaya Guru Muktananda!
Jaya Guru Muktananda!
Jaya Guru Muktananda!

PART TWO

Ashes at My Guru's Feet

INITIATION

Initiation occurs once in a lifetime.
Actions carry with them feelings and emotions.
The merits of many lifetimes, together with grace,
Bring about the divine action known as *diksha*.

The experience of initiation
Is worth every drop of life's blood.
The moment a seeker is initiated, he becomes That.
He finds a shady tree to cool himself
From the heat of worldly bondage.

When I met my Guru,
I was struck by the lightning of love.
I thought that was it, and I lived in it.
A few years later, I was struck again by that lightning.
It was then revealed to me as Shaktipat.
Once again I thought that I had come to the end of the cycle,
And I began to adapt my life to it.

That life lasted for many, many years in this world,
Though it went by in a flash.
Every second with my Guru contained a million years.

When he gave me Shaktipat,
He began his conscious work on me.
He revealed the Truth to me in many ways.

Of course, I was not always aware
Of what was being thrown in my path —
Sometimes it was love, sometimes it was envy,
Sometimes it was harsh words, sometimes it was sweetness,
Sometimes utter bliss,
Sometimes the feeling of eternal life,
And sometimes a sense of life's fleeting nature.

I did not let any one of these pass by without examining it.
I looked at it, felt it, and took care of it.

The grace of Shaktipat was omniscient and penetrating;
Whatever was supposed to stay with me remained,
And the rest was offered to the fire of yoga.
Through grace alone I was able to live
And watch as each fold of life was unfurled,
And then removed from my sight. Finally,
Everything was to dissolve into one thing: love.

Time unceasingly did its work,
Making everything except love
Vanish from before my eyes.

The subject of my taking *sannyasa*
Was brought up when I was off guard.
This was something I wanted, but it was never clear
What it would mean in my life.

I had questions: "Do I really need it?
Is it just a way to escape the world?
Is it ego or is it a gift?
Why do I need it?
Don't I already have enough labels
With which to identify myself?
Do I want yet another one to store
In the bank of my memory?"

But there was a greater power within me,
More potent than the questions and doubts.
It wanted to explode and stampede over me.
It was frightening and yet soothing at the same time.

My Gurudev let me wallow in my questions,
In my doubts.
At times he supported me;
At times he disapproved of what I was thinking.

My feelings covered such a wide range:
Sometimes divine, sometimes ridiculous.
At times I was the idol in a temple,
And at times a mere blade of grass.
Like a shy plant, I sometimes felt open,
But when the breeze of power blew in my direction,
I would close.
My Guru was compassionate
And willing to bear with me.
It was his love, it was his heart,
That allowed me to live through everything.

At last the day arrived: April 26, 1982.
My Guru sheared off my hair;
He clothed me in a white sari,
And shot the dragon's fire at me.
Maha Shaktipat took place.

For days on end I walked in that light,
Slept in that light,
Ate in that light.
Everything within and without
Was bathed in white light.
No more questions, no more doubts,
No more of those things which had gnawed at me.
I was gone.
I don't know how I left;
I only know that grace took me away
And began to install *purno'ham*.

The final day arrived: May 8, 1982.
Not much remained to be killed.
There was only the physical body which had to be covered,
Not in a white sari, but in orange cloth —
The color of the fire which had been shot at me.

That morning I went to my Guru's room,
And did a full *pranam*.
I looked at him; he looked at me.
How many times can one melt
When one has already melted completely?
So much love, so much Shakti!
Did my poor body have enough strength
To contain all this?

I was told that everything would
Take place in the Yajna Mandap
At the most auspicious of auspicious times:
My Guru's birthday.

But was he ever really born
Or did he always exist?
Was all this just a game?

Why question anymore
When "I" no longer remained
To hear the answer?

I took my seat in the Yajna Mandap near the blazing fire.
My Guru was seated on his throne,
But in that place deep within me,
Near the fire, he exploded
And became everything in the universe for me.

It thundered; it poured.
The lightning bolts smiled.
Was I shattered to pieces?
Or was I in the process of becoming whole?

Initiation occurs once in a lifetime,
Although experiences are many and come at different times.

This was when *purno'ham* was installed
In place of Swami Chidvilasananda.
The perfect "I"-consciousness, *purno'ham vimarsha*,
Is the gift of the Siddhas.
My Guru, out of his compassion,
Turned base metal into gold.
Whatever remains is his work of art.
Everything happens through his grace.

His grace flows through the mantra,
Which becomes a living companion to seekers.

The *paripurna diksha*,
More complete than the complete,
Took place on this day.

There is nothing left to do
Except to sit humbly
At the feet of my Guru;
There is nothing more to say.

THE MASTER OF LIFE'S PLAY

How often you sent for me!
Yet the reasons were always hidden from me.
Every time I came
I had a strong feeling
That the reason you had called me
Was yet to be revealed to me.

I looked at you,
But you ignored my gaze.
When I asked you mentally,
You gave me a blank look.

When I became uncomfortable,
You made things easy;
But when I felt better,
You started yelling at me.

I never knew what to do before you.
If I put my feet in the water,
You didn't like it;
If I put them in the fire,
You were puzzled by my ignorant ways.

O Baba! This no, that no, this yes, that yes.
What is really no, and what is really yes?
What is a smile, and what is a frown?

You are amazing! You encompass everything!
You enact a drama, and you also watch it.

O Baba! You love it; I know you do.
The Self is the actor, the Self is the stage,
And the senses are the spectators.

My Baba is the master of this play.

BREAKTHROUGH

Life is so many things for so many people.
For one person, it is to become a householder.
For another, an ascetic.
For one, to earn more and more money.
For another, to live a life of poverty.
For one, to rejoice in violence.
For another, complete indifference.
For one, to become famous.
For another, to hide from the world.
For one, to become known by predicting the future.
For another, to become known by remaining silent.
Everyone has a different life.
And everyone has made sacrifices in so many different ways.

What is the meaning behind this life?
Who is supposed to know whom?
Is life supposed to know you,
Or are you supposed to know life?

I know one thing about my life:
The power of grace has taken me across.
While living, I have experienced the realm of death.

Offering one's life to the Master
Is the most benevolent and frightening experience.

My Guru gave me the knowledge
Of who is supposed to know whom — you or life.
Through the years that I was graced
To spend with my Guru,
I experienced one breakthrough after another.

It was definitely his grace that gave me life.
But resistance, lack of understanding,
And the inability to surrender
Created one wave after another.
I was struck by each wave and washed clean.

Each successive breakthrough
Came at the peak of intense *tapasya*,
And it was also the fruit of that austerity.
Whether it came during waking, dreaming, or deep sleep,
From the mantra, meditation, or seva,
Or from a glance, a look, or a word from my Guru —
He used everything to mold my life.

He was both tender and harsh,
Loving and rejecting, smiling and stern,
All-embracing and transcendent.

Everything that happened
Begot the self-denial
Which led to the knowledge of the Self.

The tests came in many forms;
Sometimes they struck like lightning,
And sometimes they were as smooth as flowing water.
Sometimes they were as sharp as a million needles,
And sometimes they came cloaked in absolute numbness.

What was needed at all times was
Full faith and surrender.
If the doorframe is low,
Then bend your head and walk through it.
If the sword is brandished before you,
Lower your head; otherwise misfortune will result.

So it is in *sadhana*.
Make the life that you choose to live a worthy one.
It is a matter of great fortune
To rejoice in life
Having once sacrificed it.

Life is not like an abandoned fruit,
Yet it requires absolute sacrifice.

A life without grace bears no fruit.
Millions of lives can be lived,
But for what purpose
If there is no breakthrough?
The most exquisite of all breakthroughs
Is to pass beyond the death zone of your ignorance,
To be smashed by the wave of grace
Which enfolds you in its womb,
And offers you as a sacrifice to the mantle of God.

Then life knows what you are,
And you know what life is.

ASHES AT MY GURU'S FEET

One day Baba called me,
And spoke to me sweetly.
He asked me, "Are you ready to become ashes
At the Guru's feet?" I didn't know.
I panicked and couldn't look at him.
I kept my eyes on his beautiful feet.
In my mind, I knew they were my home;
They were where I had always belonged.

Yet the question puzzled me.
With all my pride, my shortcomings, my limitations,
How would I ever become ashes at my Guru's feet?
I pranamed and took my leave of him.

The next morning after the *Guru Gita*,
A song was played throughout the ashram,
"Become Ashes at the Guru's Feet."

I froze. Was it a message?
Was it a teaching? Was it a command?
I inquired of myself, I tortured myself,
I looked very deeply within myself,
But there was no answer.

The question remained unresolved,
And my dilemma continued to grow.

The following morning I was sitting in the courtyard
Watching my beautiful Guru.
He was gentle to all who approached him.
He smiled and talked.
He observed and remained silent.

But I was not quiet.
I wondered if I was supposed to answer him,
Or if I was supposed to change.
My restlessness became unbearable.

Another day arrived.
The same inquisition took place within me.

Wandering through the ashram,
I saw a picture of Baba bowing to his Guru.
As I watched the picture, it dissolved.
In its place I saw a beautiful flame.
Baba and his Guru were within it. I wept.

To become ashes at the Guru's feet
Is to merge into the Guru.
But how could that happen?

Again Baba called me.
He looked at me lovingly,
And asked, "Have you heard the song,
'Become Ashes at the Guru's Feet?'
Isn't it the sweetest song
That you have ever heard?"

Again I was consumed by a powerful agony.
I wished I could disappear.
I wished I weren't such a rock.

All of a sudden, my Guru, my Baba,
Placed his hand on my head.
Streaks of fire exploded from his palm.
The house of my individuality was set ablaze.
Everything I had was burned away.

I wanted to save my house.
When that was impossible,
I wanted to save a few possessions.
But I could not escape —
The door of the house was also on fire.
I do not know what happened after that.

When I lifted my head from Baba's feet,
I saw through two blurry eyes
That they were wet with my tears.
My whole being was the charred remains of his love.

He began to sing,
"Become ashes at the Guru's feet."
For the first time, a smile lit up my being.
He continued to sing.

The lightning of laughter flashed between us.
We looked at each other,
And simultaneously closed our eyes in supreme agreement.
I heard him say, "You are me."
I said, "I am you."
And everything fell into the vast silence of love.

A THOUSAND MIRRORS

A thousand mirrors were neatly placed
On the table of my life.
Since life itself was an enigma,
I looked for meaning in the reflections.

Each mirror had its own width and depth
And also its own distortions.
Some reflections were smaller, and others larger;
Still others were totally out of proportion,
Yet they seemed to speak about life
And shed meaning on existence.
I watched the myriad reflections
Of feelings, thoughts, and actions.

In the beginning it was all fun,
Like a child's game —
But the game was not distant from reality.

A thousand mirrors became my dwelling.
Time passed, watching.
It seemed a comfortable way of living.

Then the Guru's grace struck my life.
One by one, each mirror was shattered to pieces.
The reality of my existence was at stake.
The table of my life was shaking.

As grace continued to strike,
Each mirror was broken into thousands of fragments,
The reflections became innumerable.
But now they no longer made sense.
Each single, clear reflection had become multifaceted.
One reflection of sadness became many.
One reflection of joy was also multiplied.
Yet nothing held true meaning anymore.

The Guru's grace continued to strike.
Ultimately, the last mirror, so dear to my heart,
The mirror which maintained the difference
Between the individual soul and the Supreme Soul,
Was about to be destroyed.

My whole being wept.
My senses abandoned me.
My world crumbled.

Destruction took its time.
While grace was penetrating deeply,
I said to myself, "People say grace is a shelter.
Why, then, am I losing all I have?"

The last mirror,
Which gave me hope,
Which gave me support,
Which held my entire universe together,
My dearest friend for lifetime after lifetime,
Was about to become the prey of grace.

The sword of light shone brilliantly.
Reflections melted in this mirror.
Finally, when the strongest mirror exploded,
Not even a trace remained
Of that existence which had once
Found meaning in reflections.

A wondrous thing had happened:
All the reflections had become grace;
All the mirrors had become grace.
Grace had revealed that everything is grace.

The Guru smiled as my non-existent life
Merged into one truth — the love of my Guru.

The table of my life had vanished;
My life itself had become the life of my Guru.

AS THE LIGHT
COMES STREAMING DOWN

As the light comes streaming down,
Yesterday, today, and forever,
The air is draped with a white robe.
The rivers seem to flow with milk.
The entire earth rejoices
With the tenderness of love.
The heart, too, expresses its thanks,
Being filled with the Lord's compassion,
With His infinite blessings.

All times are God's time,
And God's time is eternity.
Every soul knows this in its own depths,
But does not always remember what it knows.
Thankfulness is the very nature of the soul.
By not remembering that all times are God's time
You are only thankful for what seems to be good.
When you are born, it is time to thank God.
As life continues, it is time to thank God.
When you die, too, it is time to thank God.
Always this light is a blessing.
This light is compassion itself.

Today we have gathered here to celebrate
The day of Gurumayi's birth.
But how can you celebrate another's birthday
Without including yourself in the celebration?
How can you be thankful for another's life
If you are not thankful for your own?
How can you be truly part of a celebration
Without sharing in its ecstasy?

How can you love someone else.
If you have not felt your own heart?
How can you look at another with love,
If you are not in that love already?

Everlasting light streams down
Touching earth and heaven simultaneously,
Sustaining life in all three worlds.
This very light is the brilliance in words.
It is the vitality in plants and flowers.
It is the power that heals wounded hearts.
This light is the life of all.

It is possible for a heart to be thankful
Only when it realizes its infinite luminosity.
Then, whether you are passing through a dark tunnel
Or one bathed in light,
Whether you are being scorched by the noonday sun
Or anointed by a cooling balm,
Whether you are eating bitter crumbs
Or the sweetest delicacies,
Whether you are sitting on jagged coral,
Or the softest sand,
There is nothing that you cannot bear.
As the light of your heart falls on all,
Your good karma constantly returns you
To the love of your own heart.

The love of my heart is my Guru.
The power of his grace brought me back to him.
His presence on earth is the delight of my heart.
Whatever our relationship was in other lifetimes,
In this lifetime it was most certainly
The Guru-disciple relationship.

I ask God to give me enough time
To thank Him for this relationship.
In the Guru-disciple relationship
My being has become vast as well as tiny,
Manifest as well as unmanifest,
Great as well as small.
The grace of my Guru has taught my heart
To be thankful for what has been given to me
And also for what has not been given to me.

In 1975 Baba asked me to translate for him.
I did not speak English —
At least not well enough to make any sense.
So I asked him, "Baba, if you knew
I would be translating for you,
Why didn't you force me to learn English
Long ago?" He replied,
"If I had asked you to learn English before,
You would not be so thankful to learn it now.
You would have had so much time on your hands.
But now you have to learn it right away.
Every minute you will be thankful
For learning to speak the language."

I understood my Guru wanted to teach me humility.
If I had already learned the language
I would have had the pride of learning.
Instead I felt only thankfulness
For every word I could offer my Guru.

Another time, when I was still in school,
Baba told me he would celebrate
My sixteenth birthday in the ashram.
He talked about it to everyone.
He told me about the grand things he would prepare.
And the gifts he was going to shower on me.

The day before my birthday
I was supposed to go to Ganeshpuri,
But God decided to open the heavens
And send torrents of rain.
There was flooding everywhere.
No form of transportation was moving.
All night my heart was in despair.

The next day was my birthday.
I could still have gone to Ganeshpuri,
But the Lord was not done with His blessings.
The rain was still pouring.
My heart was so troubled, so grave.
It did not feel any joy
From the light streaming down.

The next weekend I went to Ganeshpuri.
My birthday was not mentioned,
And I received no belated gift.
As I pranamed to say goodbye Sunday evening,
Baba looked at me and asked,
"Did you remember me on your birthday?"

His question was an arrow
That struck the fountainhead of tears.
I realized that Baba's true gift
Was the remembrance of my Guru,
Not some external object.
And I had received the gift of remembering him.

I continually pined for my Guru —
For his love, his fierceness, his kindness,
His discipline, his generosity, his self-control,
His grace, and his compassion.
He was in every moment of my day.

As Baba asked me his question
I was riveted to the floor.
Everything melted into one bowl
Overflowing with his eternal love.
The silence was so profound!
I could not even hear the beating of my own heart.

Then Baba said, "I remembered you, also."
In the deepest silence,
Those words full of love
Opened a new dimension in my heart.

What else can I say but, "Thank you, Lord."
It is possible to count the blessings
That you understand, but how can you count
The blessings you do not understand?

Blessings are countless. Without blessings
You cannot even take a single step.
God's blessings are there,
Not only when your desires are fulfilled,
But even when they are not.
A thankful heart is aware of this.

In the Guru-disciple relationship
The Guru's compassion is the *sudarshana chakra*,
Destroying evil and protecting good.
When you are following the spiritual path,
The Guru's compassion strengthens your interest.
His compassion is revealed
In every posture of your life.

Only a thankful heart will recognize it
And experience his compassion,
Not just when you think you need it,
But at every moment of your life.
How can words convey the Guru's compassion?
It makes no distinctions, knows no bounds.

Recently, I dreamed of Bade Baba.
His huge, dark body lay on a simple mat.
I had the good fortune to massage his body.
His skin was so tender, so soft!
With great care and love I was rubbing his chest.
And I was as gentle as I could be.
I asked him why his joints were so stiff,
Why he was having so much pain.
He turned his eyes toward me,
And with the softest look
He said, "If I did not take the pain
Of those who love me, what would become of them?
This is not pain. It is their love."

His words, so filled with love,
Engulfed my entire being with infinite compassion.
No words can possibly describe what I felt.
Bade Baba was compassion incarnate.

The essence of the Guru-disciple relationship
Is the Guru's compassion.
It is limitless and unfathomable.
So subtle yet infinitely powerful,
It takes a disciple across
The ocean of birth and death.

These priceless gems —
blessings, compassion, and thankfulness —
Are given to us all without measure.
They are never taken from us.

To be worthy of experiencing profound thanks,
You must have devoted eyes,
Vision that is pure enough to perceive
The light that is constantly streaming down.

To experience God's unending blessings,
Your head must be clear.
To know the compassion that ceaselessly flows,
Your being must become like a river of milk.

THE FORM
THAT I CAN ALWAYS LOVE

In the back of the meditation hall,
In the alcove, I sat very still
As my ears heard all about the Goddess Kundalini
And my eyes perceived Her different forms on the screen.

Suddenly a bolt of energy
Shot through my body so intensely
That my entire being became motionless,
Transfixed by the picture of my beloved Guru
Behind the Guru's *gadi*.

His eyes were piercing me,
And his entire being was moving to embrace me.
It was so real!

A tender voice within me
Melodiously said to him,
"O Goddess Kundalini,
I am so happy you took this form
That I could love all my life."

And it kept repeating itself:
"The form that I can always love,
The form that I can always love,
The form that I can always love...
Which in turn takes me to the formless."

It all began in love
And remained in love.
Finally, love dissolves in love. O Baba!
When I told you I wanted to offer my life to you,
You asked me how far I would like to go.

I said, "If you could just give me grace and devotion,
I would never want to see the end of my surrender."

You beamed, stroked my head, and said,
"I could never tell you before,
But now I want you to know
You have come here because
I wanted it to be so."

When you said that, Baba,
You did something to me.
It is yet to be understood.

You are the form of God that I love.
Your form has bestowed everything.
It is through your form that I have been able
To complete the journey within myself.

Your form is grace.
Your form is love.
Your form is a blessing.
Your form is everything
I would ever want in my life.

How shall I worship you?
What hymns, what verses, what songs, what dances,
What flowers, and what fruits —
What elements must I use to worship you?

You dissolved me into your love,
So there is no more "I" and "mine."
What I have is all from you.
How can I return your own gift?

So, my beloved Baba,
If you take away the physical body
And make it merge into your form,
Which I love to this day,
Perhaps song will merge into song,
Perhaps flame will merge into flame,
And love will become love.
And that is what you are, my Gurudev.

In the *Guru Gita* I recite every day:

I remember Shree Guru who is Parabrahman,
I speak of Shree Guru who is Parabrahman,
I bow to Shree Guru who is Parabrahman,
I worship Shree Guru who is Parabrahman.

GLOSSARY

ASHRAM   A place devoted to the practices of yoga; often the residence of a spiritual Master.

BABA, OR BABAJI   Father; a term of affection for a saint or holy man.

BADE BABA   The elder Baba; refers affectionately to Bhagawan Nityananda, Swami Muktananda's Guru.

BLUE PEARL   The subtle abode of the inner Self; a brilliant point of blue light, seen in meditation.

GANESHPURI   A village north of Bombay, at the foot of the Mandagni Mountain in Maharashtra, India, where Baba Muktananda built his ashram at his Guru's command; the home of Siddha Yoga.

GURU GITA   Lit., "The Song of the Guru"; an ancient Sanskrit text which describes the nature of the Guru, the Guru-disciple relationship, and meditation on the Guru.

GURU PURNIMA   The full moon in July, celebrated as the Guru's moon.

GURU'S GADI   The seat of the Guru, invested with the power and authority of the lineage.

JAYA   An exclamation of praise, generally translated as "Hail!"

KUNDALINI   Pure conscious energy; a form of the Shakti, which lies coiled at the base of the spine in the subtle body and is awakened by the Guru.

MAHA   Great, mighty, all-powerful.

PARABRAHMAN   The formless Absolute.

PARIPURNA DIKSHA   The ultimate initiation in which the disciple receives Self-realization from the Master.

PRANA   The breath; the universal power of life.

PRANAM To bow; to greet with reverence.

PURNO'HAM Perfect "I"-consciousness; awareness of one's inner divinity.

PURNO'HAM VIMARSHA The experience of complete identity with Supreme Consciousness, within and without; awareness of the perfect "I am."

RASA Nectar, sweetness.

SADHANA Spiritual discipline and practices; the spiritual journey.

SAMADHI State of meditation; the experience of union with the Absolute.

SANNYASA Initiation into monkhood.

SEVA Selfless service; work performed with devotion and detachment.

SHAKTI The divine energy, which creates, maintains, and dissolves everything in the universe.

SHAKTIPAT The descent of grace; the transmission of spiritual power or Shakti from Guru to disciple.

SO'HAM Lit., "I am That." The sound vibration of the Self which occurs spontaneously with each incoming and outgoing breath.

SUDARSHANA CHAKRA The discus carried by Lord Vishnu to protect His devotees and destroy evil.

TAPASYA The fire of yoga; the experience of heat generated by spiritual practices; also, austerities.

YAJNA MANDAP A pavilion in the Ganeshpuri Ashram where ancient fire ceremonies, *yajnas*, are performed.

YOGA Lit., "union"; the state of oneness with the Self; the practices leading to that state.

INDEX OF FIRST LINES

FURTHER READING

BY GURUMAYI CHIDVILASANANDA
Kindle My Heart

BY BABA MUKTANANDA
From the Finite to the Infinite
I Am That
Play of Consciousness
Kundalini: The Secret of Life
Secret of the Siddhas
Siddha Meditation
I Have Become Alive
Does Death Really Exist?
Getting Rid of What You Haven't Got
Where Are You Going?
Light on the Path
The Perfect Relationship
Mukteshwari I & II
Satsang With Baba, Volumes I-V
Reflections of the Self
In the Company of a Siddha
Mystery of the Mind
Meditate

Aphorisms
I Love You
To Know the Knower
The Self Is Already Attained
A Book for the Mind
I Welcome You All With Love
God Is With You

Siddha Meditation is practiced
in more than 600 Ashrams and Centers
around the world.

For information, contact:

GURUDEV SIDDHA PEETH
P.O. Ganeshpuri (PIN 401206)
District Thana, Maharashtra, India

or

CENTERS OFFICE, SYDA FOUNDATION
P.O. Box 600, South Fallsburg, NY 12779
(914) 434-2000.